ROYAL B

Helen Orme is a successful author of fiction and non-fiction, particularly for reluctant and struggling readers. She has written over fifty books for Ransom Publishing.

Helen was a teacher for nearly thirty years. She worked as a Special Educational Needs Co-ordinator in a large comprehensive school, as an advisory teacher for IT and as teacher-in-charge for a pupil refe experiences have been in writing.

StreetWise

The Newcomer

Helen Orme

Ransom

Street**Wise**

The Newcomer
by Helen Orme

Published by Ransom Publishing Ltd.
Radley House, 8 St. Cross Road, Winchester, Hampshire SO23 9HX, UK
www.ransom.co.uk

ISBN   978 184167 332 5
First published in 2014

CONTENTS

NOTICE

ONE

Get Her!

The classroom door opened, but no one took much notice.

Until the girl walked in.

Will took one look and poked Jim.

'Get a load of that!'

'Oh, yes,' said Jim. 'I like the look of her.'

Ms Brown looked round the class.

'You can sit next to Kim for now,' she said. 'She'll look after you.'

'Kim, this is Maddison.'

Kim looked at Maddison.

'Do we call you Maddy?' she asked.

'No.'

Kim looked at Gemma, her best friend.

'Get her!' she mouthed.

Maddison looked round the room. She didn't look at the girls, but smiled at Will.

Kim thought she had better try to be friendly.

'Where are you from?' she asked.

'The States.'

Maddison looked at her as if she was stupid.

*****

All morning it was the same. Kim tried to be friendly, but Maddison just didn't want to know.

It was different at lunch-time though. Jim and Will came over to talk to them. Suddenly Maddison was all smiles. She had plenty to say to them.

TWO

What's Up?

The boys thought Maddison was great.

Not just Will and Jim, but the rest as

well.

She didn't make friends with any of the

girls though, however hard they tried.

Soon they stopped trying.

*****

After a week, Kim noticed that even

some of the boys were a bit less friendly.

'What's up?' asked Kim, when Will

walked away from Maddison.

He looked really fed up.

'Nothing's ever right with her,' he said.

'It's always … "at home it's not like this … "

She's so, I don't know – American!'

'He's right,' said Gemma. 'She doesn't like school dinners.'

'Well, who does?' said Kim.

'Yeah, well,' said Gemma. 'But she doesn't like the weather, she thinks school is boring, she thinks the shops are useless … '

'I'm with her on most of those,' said Will. 'But it's not just that – she just moans about everything. And she won't listen to anything anyone tells her.'

Gemma agreed. 'Everybody is getting fed up with her.'

'Maybe,' said Kim, who always tried to be kind to people. 'But I'm going to go on trying to be friends with her.'

THREE

Half-Term

Kim tried very hard to be nice to

Maddison. It didn't do any good though.

Maddison wouldn't talk to any of the

girls. She still got on all right with most of

the boys though, and that made the girls

even more annoyed.

*****

At last it was half-term. Kim was glad

not to have to see Maddison. She'd given

up on her, because it just caused too

much trouble.

Gemma and her other friends didn't

understand why she even tried.

*****

Kim and Gemma had been shopping.

They were both tired out.

Gemma was meeting her mum, so she

walked across the park with Kim, who

was going to catch the bus home.

They were just about through the park,

where the really posh houses started,

when Gemma looked at her watch.

'Oh no! Mum will kill me.'

'Go on back, then,' said Kim. 'I've got

loads of time before my bus.'

Gemma turned and started running

back the way they'd come.

'See you tomorrow,' she called.

Kim went out of the park and along the

road. Suddenly there was a loud crash as a

front door slammed. Kim looked round.

A girl came running out and bumped

into her.

It was Maddison.

FOUR

I Don't Need Anybody

Maddison glared at Kim. 'What are you doing here?'

Kim was going to be rude back, but then she noticed that Maddison had been crying.

'What's up?'

Maddison wiped her face with her hand.

'Nothing.'

Kim couldn't help herself. She was

always the same with people who were

hurt or unhappy.

'Come and have a coffee and tell me

about it,' she said.

'I haven't got any money,' said

Maddison. 'My purse is inside and I'm not

going back for it.'

'It's OK,' said Kim. 'My treat.'

Maddison didn't look pleased, but she must have thought that even going with Kim was better than going back indoors. She shrugged her shoulders and started walking back through the park.

*****

The park café was open and Kim got

the drinks. To her surprise, Maddison started to talk.

She hated England. She missed her friends and thought the girls at school were all mean.

Kim wanted to stick up for her friends, but she thought it would be better to keep quiet.

*****

It took quite a long time before
Maddison stopped.

She looked at Kim. 'Thanks for
listening.'

*****

Back at school, Kim looked out for
Maddison. She smiled when she saw her.
She went over to her.

Maddison turned away. Then she

turned back to Kim.

'Don't think this makes us friends,' she said. 'It doesn't. I don't need you. I don't need anybody.'

Questions on the Story

◆ Why does Maddison hate England?

◆ What does Kim do to try and make friends?

◆ How does Maddison react at the end of the story?

Discussion
Points

◆ What might have been happening in Maddison's house to make her storm out?

◆ Did the story have the ending you expected? Why do you think Maddison still doesn't want the girls' friendship?

◆ What are the main difficulties in moving to a new country?

Activities

◆ Write an email that Maddison
sends to a friend in America about
her new life.

◆ Write character studies of Maddison and Kim.

◆ Someone is moving to England.
Write an advice sheet.

Include good and bad features!